SPEAKIN' NOR[...]
AS SHE SHUD B[...]

A GUIDE TO THE LANGUAGE SPOKEN
IN THE NORTH OF IRELAND

by Doreen McBride

Published by Adare Press

ISBN 0-9516686-7-6

Typeset by December
Printed by Banbridge Chronicle

CONTENTS

ACKNOWLEDGEMENTS

Thanks are due to family, friends and acquaintances who shared many a hilarious midnight hour; to Tom Thompson from 'Bargain Books' for his helpful suggestions; to those who attended my lecture series 'Old Ways, Old Days' at the Department of Continuing Education, Queen's University Belfast; and last, but by no means least, to Gerry Anderson and to all the people who replied to my request for help on his radio show. Gerry, himself an expert Norn Iron speaker, made a valuable contribution.

INTRODUCSHUN

Irish people generally love strangers and make them feel very welcome. That's very true in the north, although we've got to admit that people coming from outside Norn Iron speak with a strange accent. They don't speak the English language as it oughta be spoke. It's very difficult to understand them. Well, after listenenin' to people from all over, and hardly understandin' wot thar tryin' to say, Ah've decided to do something about it and produce a dictsunary to help foreigners speak proper.

Yous must know that when Queen Elizabeth the first decided to plant people in Ireland, the smartest ones came to Norn Iron and there they stayed, speakin' perfect Shakespearean English, which they combined with translations of the most meaningful Gaelic. This gave rise to the most wonderful English ever invented. The average punter from Norn Iron will not budge an inch on any important issue and certainly not on anything as vital as language, so its version of English has remained – unadulterated. In other words Norn Iron has preserved the culture others need. It's only right to share it.

BRAVE AN' USEFUL WORDS

It's possible to become confused when listenin' to conversayshuns in Norn Iron because one word may have many meanings. This has advantages, after all, it's only right that time an' effort should be repaid. If trouble is taken in learning the meaning of a word and how to spell it, it ought to be used as much as possible! This shows how smart an' efficient people in Norn Iron are with the English language.

To help youse Ah've taken the time and trouble to list a few words that have more than one meanin'.

Yer man's airlocked

hic!

AIRLOCKED
to be completely drunk   he wus airlocked
stoppage in a pipe   the radiator wus airlocked

ANY
sex   she said she ain't avin' any
none   he ain't got any

BAKE
mouth   big Aggie hit him a dig in the bake

to make cakes or bread   Cissie says she's away til bake

BAP
a small loaf   them's nice baps
head   he bumped his bap

BASTE
beast   the poor baste
hit   Ah'll baste ye
pour juices over meat
cooking in the oven   Ah must baste the roast

BLATTER
  banging noise

  to hit

he hit the drum an it made a
terrible blatter
she blattered his head in

BLERT
  to constantly complain
  an annoying person

he's alwus blertin'
he's a right blert

BLOCKED
  drunk
  stoppage in a pipe

he wus absolutely blocked
them pipes is blocked

BLOW
  boast
  movement of air

he wus alwus blowin'
it wus blowin' a gale

BLU
  a primary colour
  air movement
  loud noise
  sexy
  swear words

they painted the house blu
it blu a gale
the horn's blu
he tauld a blu joke
he hit his thumb with a
hammer and made the air blu

BORD
  bird
  plank
  get on

the bords sing in the trees
give us a bord to fix this flur
the bus's leavin', ye'd better
bord

The bords sing in the trees

BRAVE

good	he's a brave wee fella
very	the Cave Hill's a brave high hill
courageous	he wus quare an' brave the way he faced her

BUCKET

to rain heavily	it wus bucketin'
a container used for carrying water	she cud carry the heaviest bucket

CALL

reason	thar's no call to worry
shout	Ah called up the stairs
visit	Ah called on ar Sammy
collect	Ah'll call for ye at seven fur the wee meetin'

CLAP

see	did ye ever clap yer eyes on the like av 'er?
put	he was clapped in jail
applaud	she got a great clap
cows' droppings	she stud in a load av cow clap
sexually transmitted disease	they caught the clap in Majorka

CLAPPERS

wooden implements for making butter	do ye see them wee clappers
go fast	they went like the clappers

CLATTER

a large number	a right clatter of people attended the meeting
a loud noise	he kicked the bucket an made a terrible clatter

CLOCK
timepiece — luk at the clock
a black beastie — Ah hate them clocks
hit — cum 'ere 'til Ah clock ye one
sit and be lazy — luk at 'er clock
hatch eggs — the hen's gone to clock
sit on the toilet — he's awa' til clock

CLOD
throw — stop cloddin' stones
a piece cut out of the earth
with a spade — he dug a lot av clods

CLOSE
warm weather — it's quare an' close
secretive — she's quare an' close
near — she held 'im close

CLOUT
hit — Ah'll gi ye a clout on th' ear
cloth — pass us thon bit o' clout

COD
joke — it's a right cod
joker — he's an auld cod
lie — that's a cod!
fish — Wee Hughie sells great cod

CRACK (CRAIC)
fun, conversation — we'd great crack last night
a little break in plaster,
a cup or glass — the cup 'ad a crack in it
open slightly — the windy was opened a crack

noise made by whip or gun — we heard the crack of the gun

not wise — yer head's cracked

CROCK

someone who is not feeling well
old fashioned container for milk

damage

Yer nathin' but an auld crock
cover yer crock wi' muslin te
keep them flies outta the milk

Ah crocked the cyar

CUT

appearance
embarrassed
not wise
injury caused by sharp
implement

ye shudda seen the cut of 'im
Ah was cut til the bone
yer head's cut

ar Sammy cut 'imself wi' a
knife

Ye shudda seen the cut of him

He was in a daze

DAZE
    stupid   he was in a daze
    24 hours   the judge gav 'im twenny daze

DEAD
    very   he's dead good at playin' the pianna; he's dead funny
    beyond help   she jist drapped dead
    hopeless   it's a dead loss

DEEP
    thoughtful, introspective   he's quare an deep
    owes a lot of money   they're deep in debt
    sulk   she's in the deep
    goes far down from the top   he drownded 'imsel in deep water

DING-DONG

sound made by a bell — Ah near died when Ah heard the bell go ding-dong

fight — they had a right ding-dong

DOH

money — they'd plenty of doh

a female deer — look at thon wee doh

opening to a house — Ma ran out the back doh

sticky mixture of flour and water from which bread is made — Ah set the doh to rise

part of the tonic solfa — Ah sed 'Sing doh, ray, me'

DROOTH

a great thirst — Ah suffered a terrible drooth

an alcoholic — he wus nothin' but an auld drooth

DUKE

get out of the way — al av yez duke

peep — she duked at him

male member of the Royal Family — Ah like the luk of the duke

DURSTEP

a very thick sandwich — luk at wee Huey tear until yon durstep

plinth before the door — Maggie, watch the durstep

FIERCE
very	it's a fierce bad day
dangerous	that's a fierce dog

GIT
amount to anything	yew ain't gonna git nowha
get	git off yer ass an git busy
rise	whin Bertie gits up in th' mornin'
clothing	ye shud av seen the git up av 'er
receive	Ah git 40 poun a week on the berrew

GLAR
stare	he did nathin' but glar
thick mud	Ah got covered in glar

HARD
opposite of soft	them sates are quare an' hard
opposite of easy	them sums are quare an' hard
employed	Ah'm hard by the Yard

HOAK
dig	they're spud hoakin'
rummage	Ah'm hoakin' in me drawers

IRON
Ireland	Norn Iron
steel like	it was made outta iron
make money	she didn't iron much
clothes smoother	yew shud iron yon shirt

LUK
look	she lukked under the bed
somebody wants you	yer lukkin'
good fortune	he's the luk o' the divil

Sure it's naybor!

NAYBOR
    someone who lives near you   meet my naybor
    no trouble   it's naybor

NORN
    none   the shap had norn av them
        wee baps left
    north   Norn Iron

RIGHT
    the opposite of left   wud ye luk at yon big one on
        the right
    near   he stud right beside 'er
    well   are ye rightly? ar ye alright?
    drunk   he wus rightly
    very   he wus rightly bluttered
    do you understand?   Ye go down thon road, then
        turn right, then left, then
        right agin. Right?

SAX
    tea time in Ballymena   we alwus 'av tea at sax
    sex   he's a sax fiend
    the number after five and
    before seven   she 'as sax brothers
    sacks   Ah can't sell me spuds cos
        Ah ain't got no sax to putt
        'em in
    saxaphone   he's great on the sax

SHUCK

    upset
    ditch usually filled with water
    the Irish sea

that shuck her
he jumped across the shuck
thar goin' across the shuck
on thar holidays

SKITE

    go out and enjoy yourself
    slap

    drops

Maisie is out on the skite
behave yourself or I'll hit ye a
right skite roun' the ankles
Ah had skites of mud aroun'
ma new boots

SNOOKER

    a game played with long poles
    and balls on a table
    prevent

Denis Taylor's a champion
snooker player
havin' big feet doesn't half
snooker ye for wearing
fashionable shoes

Ah'm snookered by ma big feet!

STEW
traditional food made from
potatoes, carrots, onions, meat   she put the stew on
it's your turn   stew ny

SPITTIN'
similar to   he's the spittin' image of his
                                  da
scolding   she was spittin' with rage
expel the contents of the mouth   he kept spittin'

Spittin' with rage.

THU
threw   she thu the taypot at him
put on   she thu on a coat
finished   I'm all thu

TIGHT
close fit   Big Aggie's blouse was too
                                  tight an' her buttons flew off
drunk   John James wus as tight as
                                  a tick
mean   he's as tight as a camel's
                                  arse in a sandstorm

TUK

stick in	tuk yer shirt in yer trousers
go away	she gave 'im a piece o' her mind, then tuk aff
remove	her feet wus killin' her so she tuk her shoes off
sew smaller	Ella's dress wus too long so 'er morr putt a tuk in it

WINE

wind	the wine blew hard
complain	she's alwus wineing
type of alcoholic beverage	she's real sophisticated, she drinks wine
high sound	the engin gave a wine

She's alwus wineing

USEFUL WORDS

A dam's wine	water
afeared	frightened
aff	off
affront	embarrass, an insult
anti-macassar	cloth, usually made of linen, used to cover the backs of chairs to keep them from being soiled

B anjaxed	completely worn out
back talk	cheeky reply
bairn	child
baloney	nonsense
bamboozle	confuse
barney	argument
bate	defeat
bawl	shout
belch	bring up stomach wind
birl	swing round
blab	tell everything
blarge	bump or crash into
blarney	idle chat
bluttered	drunk
boggin'	dirty
boke	vomit

bone shaker	any old uncomfortable means of transport such as an old bike or an old car
bra-grabber	womaniser
buff	skin
bumin'	boasting
bunkum	nonsense
butterup	flatter
buttery fingers	liable to drop things

C

adge	beg or borrow
cadger	beggar
cafuffling	courting
cafuffle	cuddle
cagey	suspicious
canny	careful, shrewd
caper	prank
carnaptious	bad-tempered
cat	short for catastrophic
chatter	talk
chatterbox	person who talks a lot
chile	child
chimley	chimney
chinwag	talk
chitter	talk
clabber	mud, dirt
clashbeg	someone who tells tales
cleave	cut

cloutie	left handed person
coddin'	joking
cog	copy
coggly	shakey
colloguing	talking
combustible(s)	food
contrairy	awkward, stubborn
corny	played out – for example, a joke
coup	knock over, fall down
cowl	cold
cowlrife	person who feels the cold
crake	nag
craiturs	creatures
craw	crow, thoat
crimped	frilled, or, regarding hair, wavy, curly
crig	testicle
croney	friend
crosspatch	peevish person
crow's feet	wrinkles around the eyes

D ab

Dab	good at doing something e.g. a dab hand
daft	crazy
dander	walk
daylights	probably 'lights' as in lungs; they knocked the daylights out of each other
diddle	cheat

dilly dally	waste time
dinge	dent, damage
dinger	going well
dishabels	old clothes
doitery	feeble or shakey
dotter	stagger around
duckle	dunghill
duffer	idiot
dunch	nudge
duncher	flatcloth hat with brim at front
dunderhead	idiot
dunt	smack or blow
dur	door

E cker

cker	school homework
eejit	fool

Yer nathin' but an eejit!

Fag   cigarette

fancy woman	mistress
farr	father
fella	fellow
fisog	face
flaff	flap about in an uncontrolled way
fleeced	robbed
foundered	cold
frizzy	small curls
fuddy duddy	stupid person
fumble	handle in an awkward fashion
funk	draw back in fear
futtin' it	walking

Gaffer   foreman

gallivant	run around
galore	plenty
gaunch	idiot
gape	stare at
gawky	awkward
geg	joke
gensey	pullover
gie	give
girn	complain
gleek	glance

gloaming	twilight
glower	glare
gorb	greedy person
gowl	howl
griskens	pieces of pork
gub	mouth
gulder	shout loudly
gumption	common sense
gunk	disappoint
gutties	old fashioned training shoes

Hackles

Hackles	feelings of anger
hafun	measure of whiskey
hallion	rascal
hap	wrap up warmly in clothes or blankets
hanel	handle
harpie	woman who constantly nags
hassle	bother
haul	pull
headbin	stupid person
headbombadeer	boss
headstaggers	confused state
head-the-ball	see headbin
herple	hobble or limp
highfalutin	affected
hives	itchy spots
hurded	bossed

Jag   prick

jap   splash

jaunt   go out and enjoy oneself

jing-bang   a number of people

jitters   feel nervous

Killinchy muffler   big hug

Loanin'   lane

Mitch   play truant

ming   smell

mizzle   very light rain

moer   mother

muffler   scarf

Neuck   steal

Oxter   armpit

Pech	gasp or pant
pishin'	raining heavily
poke	ice cream cone
Screwy	stupid
skite	go out and enjoy oneself
slabbergub	person who is talking nonsense
smite	hit
stooley	see clashbeg
Thuotha	careless

Yer thuotha

USEFUL PHRASES

Ah got a quare gunk	I had a terrible shock
Boys a dear that bates all	I'm very surprised
Come on, on in	You're very welcome
Dead on	Great, very accurate
Hold yer tongue	Be quiet
How's about ye (often shortened to 'bout ye')	How are you?
It's stickin' out	It's excellent
It's wheeker	It's excellent
On the berrew	Obtaining benefit from the social services, such as unemployment benefit
Whar the big nobs hang out	Gents' toilet
Would you like a wee cup of tea in yer hand?	Would you like some tea?
Yous gettin'?	Are you being served?
She's a haveral	She's big, brawny and awkward
S'ony me	It's only me
Splittin' yer sides	Laughing
Weel gup	We will go up

NORN IRON EXPRESSHUNS

Strangers to Norn Iron will find that the English language is spoke in a more expressive way than anywhere else. This makes the words become alive and more interestin' to thar listener. For instance, strangers might say a man 'always carried a lot of money', A Norn Ironer could say 'he alwus had a wad o' notes fit to choke an elephant.' Or a stranger might describe a girl as 'tall' while a local, especially one from County Armagh, might say 'she cud ate hay outa a laft'.

A few expresshuns commonly used throughout Norn Iron have been compiled so visitors can improve their use of the spoken word. This will aid understandin' when talkin' to locals and perhaps some of our sayings will be taken back home to amaze others who will be astounded at their intelligence. Hopefully this work will larn strangers how til spake proper.

Ah cud cry with my feet so Ah cud, thar so sore

Ah cud have soaped me ass and slid all the way to Newry and back in the time that it tuk

Ah'm sick, sore and tired of …

Ain't got enough sense to come in out of the rain

As rare as hen's teeth

As thuotha as Maggie Moore's

Black as the ace av spades

Blind as a bat

Broad as a barn beam

Busy as a bee

Cauld as a morr-in-law's heart

Clean as a whistle

Clumsy as a bull in a china shop

Clumsy as an ox

Crazy as a lune

Crooked as a dog's (donkey's) hind leg

Cud drive mice through a crossroads

Cudn't hit a cow on the ass with a bake board

Dead as a doornail

Drunk as a lord

Dry as a bone

Dull as dish water

Faster than greased lightnin'

Fat as a match

Happy as a pig in mud

Hard as nails

He goes thru toast like a cyclone

He'd luk a gift horse in the mouth he's that suspicious

He riz perches so he did, he was that shocked

High as a kite

Hoppin' mad

Hot as hell

If ye'd brains ye'd be dangerous

It's so cold it'ud freeze the balls off a brass monkey

It' ud make yer glass eye water

It wuz like showin' a red flag to a bull

Knife's so blunt it wudn't cut butter

Leppin' like a March hare

No bigger than a sparrow's fart

Right as rain

See yew, if ye fell in manure ye'd come out smellin' av roses

See yew, yer a wee wildbee

See yew, yer so thin ye'd drop down a gratin'

Sharp as a mother in law's tongue

She died with all her fasillites

She's great value

Sly as a fox

Small but beautifully marked

So tired I'm dead on my feet

Soft as a baby's bottom

Stiff as a board

Stiff as a starched shirt

There's more meat on a butcher's pencil

Tha're so straight laced they'd never make love standin' up in case they enjoyed it and started to dance

They're so unreasonable they'd not let ye luk out of yer eyes

These aul' boots are on their last legs

Ugly as sin

Wallet full of notes fit to choke an elephant

Wet as a drowned rat

Wicked as a weasel

Ye'll be the quare pup when ye grow a tail!

THREATS AN' INSULTS

Ah'll clip yer lugs, so Ah will

Ah'll av ye goin' roun' lukkin' a face transplant

Ah'll gi ye a good dig on the gub, so Ah will

Ah'll rearrange that face av yours

Ah'll take yer two ears an putt them were yer mouth is

Ah'll thump the linin' outta ye

Awa' an' suck an egg

Awa' an feel yer head

Catch a grip on yerself

Catch yerself on

Do ye want to feel the full weight of my hand?

Ye shud larn til av a titter av wit

I'd like to fix yer face

Is yer da still pullin' the wrinkles outta tripe for a livin'?

Shove it up ye … sideways

Watch yer face in case I shove it thru the back of yer neck

Watch yerself man, jest watch yerself

Y'ain't the full shillin'

Y'av a wee want

Ye av nae a gleed av sense

Yer away in the head

Ye'd drive a body bananas

Ye haven't an ounce (of sense)

Ye make my stummick turn

Ye wud, wud ye? Yew and what army?

Yer as thick as champ

Yer face'll luk like a welder's glove when A've finished with it

Yer no worth a rap

Yer nathin' but a born blert

Yer nathin' but a slabber

Yer nathin' but a wee light weight, so yar

Yer nathin' more than a parcel av bad meat

Yer face luks like my behind

Yer head's a marley

Yer just actin' the goat

Yer ma's a hamster

Yer ma's yer da

Yer not all there

Yew've a slate missin'

Yew've a tongue fit fer clippin' hedges

Yew'd do well in Crufts

Yer head's a marley

IN PRAISE OF WEEMEN

The following expresshuns describe a tall, strong woman who is able to work around a farm. That's wot a fella wi sense wants. Luks fade and strength's an asset.

Remembra a great girl cud

ate hay outta a laft
use 'er back til pull a plough
draw turf like a donkey
carry two buckets av water

A fat partner is an asset becos it shows either yew or she has enough money to ate sufficient to put on beef. Forgit slimmin'. A good woman is beef to the ankles like a Mullingar heifer.

she's a wee cracker (humdinger or wheeker)	she is wonderful
she's jist a big knock	her attractions are a bit too obvious
she's jist a wee doll	she is very pretty

If yew feel like goin' the way of most men and marryin', say:

I'd like to push yer wheelbarrow	I'd like to marry you
Wud ye like to be buried wi our folks?	Will you marry me?

DEROGATORY TERMS ABOUT WEEMEN

she's no great shakes	I don't think much of her
she's no up to much	I don't think much of her
she's not one of last year's chickens	she's getting old
she's no chicken	she's old
she'll no tear in the pluckin'	she's old
she's jist got a pullet's head	she's old
she's mutton dressed as lamb	the clothes she's wearing were designed for a younger person

She's no chicken

ABOUT MEN

he's jist a big hunk — he's very attractive

he's cuttin' a quare dash — he looks great

he's quare crack — he's great fun

he's a quare court — he's a good lover

thar no flies on him — he's clever

he's a powerful cheek — he's too forward

he's a power o' money — he's wealthy

He's a power o' money

he lives in clover — he's wealthy

he's stoney broke — he's poor

he's down at heel — he's poor

he hasn't wot wud jingle on a tombstone — he's poor

he's bummin' his load — he's boasting

he's many nicks in 'is horn — he's older than he says

the storm's liftin' his thatch — he's going bald

EXPRESSHUNS OF DISTRUST

Ar yew takin' a han out o' me?	Are you making fun of me?
Ar yew takin' a rise out o' me?	Are you making fun of me?
Ah'll no swalley that one	I don't believe you
Do ye think Ah came up the Bann in a bubble?	Do you think I'm stupid?
Go on with you	I don't believe you
Get away o' that	I don't believe you
He tuk me in	He cheated me
That takes me to the fair	I don't believe you

Ar yew takin' a rise out o' me?

TALKING ABOUT THE WEATHER

Thar many suitable expresshuns in Norn Iron to fit any occashun. As beginners studying the language it's useful to know it's always correct to talk about the weather. This allows yew to start conversayshuns with purfect strangers which will then develop in interesting ways yew will not expect.

In Norn Iron, when yew meet people in the street, especially in country towns, yew ar likely to be bowled over by thar friendliness. Purfect strangers ar likely to stop yew and proclaim 'Thar's no hate.' This refers to disgust at the awful weather rather than feelings of love. To help yew Ah've compiled a list of sayin's about the weather. They may be used in polite conversayshun or as greetings and ar useful to larn as they av a dual purpose.

DESCRIPTIONS OF THE WEATHER

Thar's no hate	It's very cold
It'ud freeze the balls uv a brass monkey	It's very cold
It'ud founder ye	It's very cold
It'ud skin ye	It's very cold
It's quare an' bitter	It's very cold
It's quare an' coul	It's very cold
It's spittin'	There's a light shower
It's a saft mornin'	There's light rain
It's only a wee skiff	It's going to be a light shower for a short time
Thar's a bit av a drizzle	There's light rain
It's a great day for ducks	It's a very wet day
It ain't half cumin' down	It's raining heavily
It's bucketin'	It's rainin' heavily

If ye can see the hills it's goin' to rain, if ye can't see 'em it's raining

(OLD SAYING)

LOST?

If a stranger becums lost in Norn Iron the most sensable thing to do is find a native and ask for directions. Remember, Norn Iron, in spite of the troubles, has the lowest crime rate in Europe. That is offishal EC statistics, not local blarney. The natives ar not only helpful, but franly. The only difficulty is unnerstannin' them, but then, that's wot this book is for.

Nobudy in Norn Iron worth his or her salt is likely to say anything as unimaginative as 'Go down that road and take the first on the right, travel half a mile, then take the road to the left.' A Norn Iron native, in common with those from the South, is more likely to point in the correct direction and say something like, 'Do you see thon beg tree down there on the left? Well ignore it, jist past it there's a wee small road on the right. Go down there til ye cum til a cross roads. Ignore thon cross roads, jist go straight thru til ye cum to a wee shap on yer lef. Drive past thon wee shap til ye see a big white bungalow. Go past the bungalow an' tek the next road on your lef.'

People from Norn Iron, in their eagerness to help strangers and make sure they unnerstan instructions, may insert the word 'right' when givin' directions. 'Do you see thon road? Right? Turn left thar. Right? Now go down thon road til ye cum til a crossroads. Right? Turn lef at the crossroads. Right? An its the third wee house on yer lef. Right?'

FEELING ILL?

Ah feel as if Ah've one fut in the grave	I feel as if I'm dying
Ah'm dead beat	I feel very tired
Ah'm frazzled	I feel very tired
Ah'm knackered	I feel very tired
Ah'm no at meself	I don't feel well
Ah'm quare an' bad	I feel awful
Ah'm run down	I haven't been feeling well lately
Ah'm that wake Ah haven't a leg unner me	I feel very weak
Ah'm far through	I'm very ill
Ah've bin lyin' a quare while	I've been ill in bed for a long time
Ah'm lyin' with the dactar	I'm ill, in bed and being attended by the doctor
Ah'm foundered	I'm cold (or hungry)
Ma hed's splittin'	I've a sore head
Ah'm in bed wi' ma hed	I'm in bed because I've a sore head
Ah'm a bit down	I'm depressed
Ah'm down in the mouth	I'm depressed
Ma stummick's turnin'	I feel sick
Ma insides are awa wi' the band	My stomach is upset
Ah'm hangin' on the mantelpiece wi' ma stummick	My stomach is upset
Ah had a gastrik flu that tuk the heels av me	I had a bad dose of gastric flu
She's in danger av distinction	She's critically ill

Ah've a wee touch av lumbago

She's waitin' on	She's dying
She got away	She died
Ah've a wee touch av lumbago	I have lumbago
Ah'm middlin'	I could feel better
Ah've a wee whinge in ma knee	My knee is aching
Ma beg toe's bin givin'me gyp fur years	My big toe has been sore for a long time
Another clean shirt'll do ye	You're not long for this world
Ah'm no feelin' too hot cos Ah'm far too warm	I'm feeling unconfortable because the temperature is too hign
Ah jist stayed in bed til Ah got up	I stayed in bed until I recovered
Cud ye set up an' ate an egg	Are you feeling better.
Ah'm cumin' til	I'm feeling better
Ah'm up the chute	I don't feel well or I'm pregnant
Ah'm up the bubble	I'm pregnant

USEFUL EXPRESSHUNS FOR THEM AS FEELS THAR MAKIN' PROGRESS

Were ye born in hospital with swingin' doors?
or
Were ye born in a fie. with the gate open?

I wish you would shut the door when you enter or leave the room

That'll harden yer groin

That's hard luck

T'was well intil the night afore Ah fell over, so it was

I lay awake fora long time before I eventually fell asleep

Ah gae ma kyar a wee dunt but she just gae a wee wheezle an' conked out

My car won't start

It's quare an' dear

That article is too expensive

Please lave no mor milk as Ah'll be awa til Ah get back

I want to cancel the milk because I'm going away from home for a few days

Wild horses wudn't make me

No! I won't

Wud ye bek? Bek yer kyar or ye'll end up in the shuck. Bek awa forward

Reverse your car or you'll end up in the ditch. Reverse

DIFFICULT EXPRESSHUNS FOR ADVANCED STUDENTS ONLY

NORN IRON'S 'WEE'

Strangers to Norn Iron find correct use of the word 'wee' extremely difficult. In the context of Norn Iron it is very important. A lot of subtle meaning is given to the word by the tone in which it is uttered. This is difficult for outsiders to master but is vital if one is to larn to spake Norn Iron as she shud be spoke.

'Wee' may be used to convey the concept of small size, as in 'Yur quare an' wee'. Locally it is considered correct to add the word 'wee' to emphasise the idea of small size such as in 'I'd like a little wee small dram o' whiskey' or 'Luk at that little wee small lad!' or 'She lives in a wee small house'.

The word 'wee' may also be translated as 'nice' as in 'Wud ye like a wee cup o'tea?' or 'How about a wee pint o' the black stuff?'

'Wee' may be used as a term of endearment, as in 'Yew poor wee sowl' or 'Poor wee Sammy'.

Another meaning of 'wee' is 'short' as in 'Ah'm goin' fur a wee walk' or 'Ah'll only be a wee while'. This type of use of the word wee is extremely difficult becos a lot depens on the way the word is said. The 'wee walk' cud be a few yards or several miles, the 'wee while' might mean a few minutes or several hours. In the same way a 'wee bit of a girl' cud mean a nice quiet young woman or somebody pretending to be something she isn't, and a 'wee bit o' a laugh could mean a hilarious night out or a mild chuckle. The only advice which may be given is to WATCH carefully and draw yer own conclusions. Rememba, practise makes purfect.

THOWL

'Thowl' is a simpler word to use correctly than 'wee'. A rough translation of 'thowl' is 'the old'. This may be either a term of affection or abuse so watch the speaker and translate the word in context.

We're awa to see thowl aunts

EXAMPLES OF 'THOWL'

Ah'm awa te see thowl aunts	I'm going to see my mother's (or my father's) sisters
thowl man	husband, may also mean father or an old man
thowl woman	wife, may also mean mother or an old woman
thowl fella	see 'thowl man'

'Thowl' may be inserted in front of parts of the body, as in 'thowl beck's givin' me gyp' (my back's sore) or 'thowl feet ar killin' ma' (my feet are very sore).

Lizzie wus a grate thowl girl. If she hadda lived she wud av been a hunderd. (Lizzie probably died a long time ago but the speaker is expressing a lot of affection for her.)

Shuey wus a grate thowl fella. If he hadda lived til Friday he'd av been dead a fortnight. (The speaker is expressing affection for Hugh, often pronounced 'Shuey'. The above sentence is a common mode of expresshun. It keeps listeners on their toes and develops intelligence.)

SOME PHRASES FUR ADVANCED STUDENTS

Ah haven't ma teeth in and Ah'm talkin' upside down
(Excuse me, I feel I have expressed myself badly)

Ah was in ma dishabeals puttin' on the tea when there was a knock at the door an' there was the curate. I was fairly put on.
(I was dressed in my old clothes preparing a meal when the curate came to the door and I felt embarrassed)

Ah'm all behind in ma front
(My front garden needs attention)

If ye were any sharper ye'd cut yerself
(The translation of the above phrase requires powers of observation and understanding of the circumstances in which it was uttered. It could be a compliment as when commenting on a particularly sharp piece of wit, or it could be an insult regarding sharp practise.)

The nixt time Ah see thon wee targe Ah'll give 'er a gud joinin'
(The next time I see her I'll tell her I disapprove)

Ah put ma feet up for five minutes an' fell over.
(I was tired so I lay down meaning to doze for five minutes but I fell asleep)

ALSO PUBLISHED BY ADARE PRESS

Stand Up And Tell Them
October 1991, 80pp, £4.99
ISBN 0-9516686-2-5
Hilarious monologues by Crawford Howard, Billy Ritchie and Maud Steele.

Stand Up And Tell Them Some More
November 1991, 80pp, £4.99
ISBN 0-9516686-4-1
More hilarious monologues by Crawford Howard, Billy Ritchie, Seamus Lavery and Bill Nesbitt.

A Sense of Love A Sense of Place
November 1992, 80pp, £4.99
ISBN 0-9516686-5-X
Stories associated with places in Northern Ireland, as told by John Campbell, Tom McDevitte, Cecil Brennan and other well known yarnspinners. These stories were first broadcast on Radio Ulster's *Love Forty* programme.

LOCAL BOOKS FOR CHILDREN

Ceri the Celtic Cow
by Doreen McBride
May 1992, 16pp, £2.99
ISBN 0-9516686-3-3
Life and times of the Celts as seen through the eyes of a rather special cow. Contains pictures to colour, suggestions for places to visit and things to do.

Susan's Rabbit
by Seamus Lavery
Forthcoming November 1993
ISBN 0-9516686-6-8
Story in verse about a little girl who took her pet rabbit to school. This story caused the phone lines to the BBC to be jammed when it was broadcast on the Gerry Anderson Show.